Station Hunting on the Warrego

Station Hunting on the Warrego:

AUSTRALIA:

AT THE VALLEY OF THE POPRAN

AND

OTHER POEMS,

BY

PHILIP J. HOLDSWORTH.

Sydney

WILLIAM MADDOCK, 381 GEORGE STREET.

1885

From the author, to his
dear and valued friend
Thomas Butler Esq.
of the Sydney University,
with perennial regards.

R. J. H.
19
10

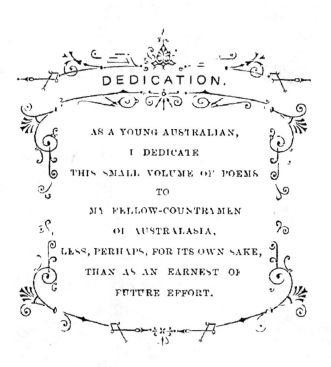

DEDICATION.

AS A YOUNG AUSTRALIAN,

I DEDICATE

THIS SMALL VOLUME OF POEMS

TO

MY FELLOW-COUNTRYMEN

OF AUSTRALASIA,

LESS, PERHAPS, FOR ITS OWN SAKE,

THAN AS AN EARNEST OF

FUTURE EFFORT.

Contents

Sonnet

TO NORTH HEAD—SYDNEY HARBOR.

Above thy crest, the shimmering sea-bird screams,
And wheels and hides with countless, white-winged flocks,
'Mid rifts and clefts that gap thy splintered blocks '—
Below—where mottled Ocean swirls and gleams,
(And moans like one perturbed by troublous dreams)
The cold, white surge, with melancholy shocks,
Hums dirges amid grey, fantastic rocks !

     O strong sea-rampart ! whose stern grandeur mocks
The baffled aims that fret me, till Life seems
A pendulum that swings 'twixt Grief's extremes,—
And Time a deep, sad, tomb for cherished schemes—
Would God—(since days fall foul, and glad things flee,)
My yearning soul could pluck strange strength from thee,
To front the World's inexorable sea !

Australia.

A RHAPSODY

O MUSE divine! within whose strange soft lyre
  Melodious lays of subtle strength and splendor
Sleep, till the Bard's quick touch and tongue of fire
  Lure them to life ·—Even Thou, sweet Muse, engender
Within my brain, songs passionate and tender—
Songs sung or harped 'mid thy most secret spheres,
But snatched by amorous couriers to mine ears,
And hoarded in my soul's most hallowed cells
(Where the mute seraph, Contemplation, dwells)
        Till the renascent hour,
        When, summoned by thy power,
Dainty and swift once more their melody outwells

I

Australia! he that anthems thee aright
        Must psalm his loud delight
With lips of gold, and supple tongue as pure,
And sounding harp, than mine less immature!
Yet, should my happy verse, though faint, refuse
        To trumpet forth thy dues,

Methinks dumb trees (each leaf a tongue of flame!)
Would clarion out thy grandeur, and my shame:
Thy timorous vales responsively would hymn
      Like sweet-lipped cherubim—
Each peak would lift its sky-saluting crest
      Still loftier from earth's breast,
And blend, with melting murmurs, into strong
      Ambrosial breaths of song ·
Yea, vehemently plead to listening earth
The perfect marvel of thy matchless worth!

II.

Thrice hail the bright day when the refluent sea
      Witnessed the birth of thee!
When, from dark, solemn, depths of foam-fringed surge,
Mysterious and divine, thou didst emerge,
Framed, by God's grace, that after-years might see
A sacred shrine, thrice dear to Liberty!
On that glad day (O best-born day of Time!)
God gathered rare delights from each fair clime,
And scattering them with bountiful High Hand,
Most lavishly they rained on thee O Land!
Such was the ripe wealth of the prodigal dower
      That decked thy natal hour!

III.

Yet, like some magic scroll,

　　Which no man dare unroll.

Enchantment veiled thy beauties, while sublime

And shadowy epochs scaled the steeps of Time ,

Till the brave mariner, with bounding ships,

　　Clove, through green Sea's foam-lips,

To where thy tranquil splendors slept, impearled,

And, from obscure recesses, called a Second World.

IV.

Thine was the trumpet-tongue, illustrious Cook,

　　That roused Mankind, and shook

Blind, brooding, Ignorance from Austral waves,

And drove her, darkling, to far dungeon-caves !

　　Thine was the hand that found,

　　And valiantly unbound,

The long-closed Volume of our land's delight,

And bared the priceless wealth thereof, in all men's sight.

V.

For this, O chief of Ocean's pioneers,

Thy dauntless deeds make music in our ears—

　　(Outsinging all thy peers!)

For this, just Memory, heedful of great acts,
    Imperially enacts
That, in her clearest chronicle, loud Fame
    Shall glorify thy name!
(A shining tribute which few kings can claim!)

VI

Dear land! above whose hills, and vales, and streams,
Joy swoons, delirious, rapt with honeyed dreams!—
    Thou hast no storied plains,
Thick-strewn with shattered palaces and fanes—
No old-world wrecks, which prate to distant times
Of perished pomps, and records red with crimes.
    And thy clear springing waters,
Unbeaconed with the blood of human slaughters,
    Haste, garrulous with glee,
To mix full treasures in one placid sea!
    Nor hast thou viewed the baleful day
    When phalanxes, in mailed array,
    Spurred by the hate that Vengeance hoards,
Shook the sharp clamors from their clashing swords
    And bade the foe, with blow and thrust,
    Bite the blind, suffocating dust—
Till Virtue trembled from her god-like seat,
And, wailing, fled with faint, reluctant feet.

VII.

For round thy broad, delectable expanse,
Soft Peace broods, sweetly, in celestial trance ;
  While, quiet and benign,
Unnumbered synods of winged joys combine
To guard, with gracious care, thy prospering State
From rough, rude brawls, and travelling tongues of hate !

VIII.

O Austral hills, and dim delightful dells !
O boundless plains, made glad with fruitful things !
O storm-worn clifts, whose stern, stark, front repels
The surge that spins aloft on soft white wings !
O sleepless clamors of sea-thunderings !
Straight through your realms let one triumphal chant
  Ring,—swift and jubilant !
Even from the sea, to where lone, swirling, plain s
(Remote from grovelling cits, and stolid swains !)
Stretch, for fantastic leagues, their drear domains—
Lift your high anthems—till dull Man confess
(Right volubly) my land's rare loveliness ;
And trump, in tones that none dare controvert
A World's loud homage to her rich desert !

At the Valley of the Popran:

HAWKESBURY RIVER

Where hurrying Popran slides and leaps
Past white, smooth, sands, and stubborn steeps,
Or glides through green arcades—whose trees
(Branch-tangled) weave strange bowers to please
This traveller toward abysmal seas—
I loiter!——

From the grove's heart comes,
(Grave-voiced, like oceanic hums,—)
God's mystic forest-rhyme, that dumbs
And drowns the blare o' the world.

                                   Above,
The wonga, myrtle-perched, coos love,
And petulant red-bills, fleet-winged, free,
Prattle their magic minstrelsy !

Hark, haply from yon black-butt's height,
Small yellow-bosomed bell-birds smite

Crisp air with clarions of delight!—*
O bell-bird! happy bird! that shrills
Strong trumpet-tones where tongueless rills
And lustrous pools, fern-nooked, perdu,
Lurk—hid from all—save God and you!—
O joyful sprite! whose strains unbar
Song-treasures, filched, perchance, from far
Star-realms where spiritual dearth
And anguish vex not as on earth!—
Strong transport whirls me, as your grand
Hymns climb yon mountainous hills that stand
Like monstrous outlooks to the land!
Ah! if to me your jubilant chant
Seem Mirth's mellifluous ministrant,—
What whirlwind-joys must needs seize him
Who, lost mid labyrinths dire and grim,
With hazards near,—with helps remote,—
And Hell's thirst dominant in his throat,—

---

* The bell-birds are the poets of the brooks. Frequenting the shady streams and hidden watercourses, they fill the fragrant forest air, at times, with a miraculous monotone of strange richness and liquidity. Many a time have the distant notes of these little winged water-beckoners piloted the parched wayfarer to unseen, acceptable, waterpools; and, for this reason, even the prosaic shingle-splitter loves them.

P. J. H.

Hears—hails,—your lyric pilot-note !
May God, when fowlers range your land,
Baffle each rough churl's murderous hand !

Thus hedged, where clustering vine-shrubs climb
Past storying boughs to spheres sublime,—
Quick drift-winds (blown through odorous plots)
Steal sweets from blossoming clumps and grots,
Till, stored with pillaged perfumes, clipt
From wattle, beech, and eucalypt,—
Their strange, fresh, fragrance balms my sense
As though Heaven's bounteous Providence
Showered driblets of Sabean spice
To dower this tranquil Paradise.

Yes, canopied even here, mid throngs
Of huddling scents and passionate songs,—
And lulled by motherly PEACE, whose furled
Plumes shroud me from the turbulent world,
My happy soul, grown rhythmic, sings
These tributary anthemings ·—

Hymn to Peace.

O gracious Peace ! whose prodigal gifts make light
Dead strifes and perished toils,—dear Nymph, bedight

With maiden comeliness,—and girt with grace
In queen-like mien and face,—
Beneath thy sceptered sway Heaven lightly sets
Green, shadowy, groves, and rippling rivulets ;
And pure, cold breadths where broadening lakes expand
Yield fealty to thine hand,—
Here, where cool springs, and bubbling rills rejoice
Like lullabies, (smooth-lisped,) thy slumbrous voice
Creeps softly through the tremulous air, replete
With subtle tones and semitones more sweet
Than woodland warblings piped by small, bright birds,—
Or winsome low of herds—
More witching than the nectarous speech that slips
From love-enamoured lips—
More pure than seas whose swift stupendous shocks
Lash congregated rocks,—
More calm than moonless nights, when scarce one breath
Stirs from its sleep of death,—
As tuneable as streams, and storms, and seas,
Ay, tunefuller thrice, Supernal Peace, than these !

Lo ! years draw nigh, when, by thy might divine,
Rude Wars shall cease, and ravenous fiends malign,
With frenzied rage, and tempest-clamor start

From Earth's tormented heart!—
Yes, years approach, when Man shall feel once more
Heaven's own miraculous impress, which of yore
Transformed him from a lifeless carven-clod
To Man,—a visible God!—
Then Right, not Might, shall rule through earth's fair zones,
Possess proud realms, and buttress mighty thrones—
And cheer glad myriads mid the bland careers
Of long predicted years,—
Then Man,—new-born,—shall start from tomb-like sleep,
August, sublime,—nor crouch like beasts that creep;—
Shall spring erect,—and gather grace and strength,
While swift Time (mellowing into bliss at length)
Shall crown his being with thy boon, O Peace,
Till Death bid Life surcease!—

———

I pause! Day droops :—and, with the Day,
My song's strange effluence wastes away!
Light dwindles !—Where far hill-peaks rise,
Earth's last gold torch of sunset dies,—
While, mid deep glens, dun Eve's obscure
Hand paints Night's mimic portraiture.—
Even yet, the Alchemist Sun beguiles

High West with glorious cloudlet isles
Whose opalescent splendors gleam
Like Iris-hues in yon still stream.

Lo! moist glooms fold me .—As I stir,
Crushed rosewood leaves ooze fumes of myrrh—
(Exuberant fumes) that scent and cling
Round hands which wreak their ruining,—
(So Martyrs, panged with death-pains, pray
God's benison on them that slay!—)

Now halts my Hymn .—The stately trees,
(The quivering, multitudinous, trees!)
Stirred to the roots i' the Dusk's chill breeze
Rustle grand twilight-liturgies,—
Now dies my Hymn :—see, threading groves
Wherein no venomous fanged thing roves—
Housewards, and disenchained, I plod
'Neath stars that mystically nod
And tremble at Thy glance, O God.

The Quid Pro Quo of the Inebriate.

A DRAMATIC DIALOGUE.

INEBRIATE SPEAKS.—

In the Spring of my life, ere the vigor of pulsing blood slacked in
    my veins,

Ere my weary soul wailed with unrest, or existence grew arid with
    pains,

Youth dreamt me the dream of a Future, which Time never strove
    to destroy

Till thy merciless strength marred my peace, and made wreck of
    my limitless joy.

Yea!—while Hope's ringing voice chanted pæans that spurred me
    with lofty desires,

My luminous landscapes and vistas were scorched by thy naptha-
    line fires,—

Till, as stubble that wastes in the furnace, Hope died, and the
    promptings of Fame,

And my soul, in its bitter abasement, was thrust amid suffering
    and shame '

With the garb and sweet speech of a Grace,—with the honey of
    flattering prayers,

Thou didst strive to the uttermost span to inveigle my sense in
    thy snares,—

And thine eloquent subtleties sped,—till I fathomed the depths of
    thy spell,

To find that earth's rose-paths of pleasure converged to the
    Caverns of Hell.

Thou hast filched, from once-sinewy limbs, all the manifold strength
    of strong thews,

Till my manhood has melted away as Night melts in impalpable
    dews;

And the bleak hours that measure my life are a prey to unspeak-
    able pains!

Cease! cease! O insatiate of Spoilers!—

DEMON SPEAKS:—

                   Man! yield what remains!

INEBRIATE SPEAKS:—

Right glad fell that happiest of days when my bride claimed a
    home in my heart,

And besought that, betwixt our desires, not a thorn of contention
    should start;

When the tremulous "yea" of her speech smote with rapture the
    sombre church-aisles,

And my future of bliss seemed established, and blessed by ineffable
 smiles,

But Havoc swooped down, for thy thraldom stamped out all my
 loi dlier sense,

Till my vision was bleared with thy glamour,—my path blocked
 with rocks of offence,

And the avenues—Pity and Sorrow—that lead to Man's springs
 of remorse,

Seemed shut, O thou pitiless fiend, while I venomed Love's life at
 its source.

Yea! she ate of the bread of Affliction, and drank of Grief's
 ultimate drains !

Cease ! cease ! O insatiate of Spoilers !

DEMON SPEAKS :—

       Man ' yield what remains !

INEBRIATE SPEAKS ·—

Two children—twin blossoms of beauty—left Heaven to reflower
 by my side,

God sent them for waymarks of comfort, when mournfuller times
 should betide.

Ah, my soul soared triumphant with rapture,—for love was a lamp
 to my life

In the days ere thy malice had filled me with anguish and discord
    and strife.

O frantic, O poisonous thirst ' While those babes were of innocent
    years

Their days grew more bitter than wormwood,—their nights grew
    sad vigils of tears,

Till they withered like lilies that perish, being battered by ruinous
    rains !

Cease ! cease ! O insatiate of Spoilers !

DEMON SPEAKS.—

Man ! yield what remains !

INEBRIATE SPEAKS '—

Thou hast made me a shameful derision, till my soul grovels pros-
    trate in dust,

I am proverbed with tauntings by fools, and contemned as unclean
    by the just.

Like a madman, that frenziedly scatters sharp arrows, and fire-
    brands, and death,

I have trampled the hearts of my household, and scourged with
    my pestilent breath ;

As a waif driven wild by Hell's whirlwinds, I am wrecked on the
    drunkard's due shoals,—

A passionate theme to move laughter in Demons, and tears in saved souls.

Avaunt! for my Memory sinks blasted with Sin's ineffaceable stains!

Cease! cease! O insatiate of Spoilers!

DEMON SPEAKS —

Man! yield what remains!

INEBRIATE SPEAKS.—

I am lost! Lo, the gulfs of Destruction yawn, seething and furious below,

Alive as with infinite wails, and lamentings and mourning and woe!

Shall I quaff? Yea; though Destiny damn me with them that gnash teeth in the Pit;

I drink! though my agonized soul be eternally tortured for it.

I drink? Yea, the slave of thy chalice, I drain to the dregs of thy spell

Till unplacable Death bid me traverse the long lurid flame-tracts of Hell!

Lost! Lost! Ah, my God-banished spirit! Ah, House of Unquench-able Pains!

Cease, *now*, O insatiate of Spoilers! *Thou hast what remains!*

Station Hunting on the Warrego.

AN EPISODE OF AUSTRALIAN FRONTIER LIFE.

(Just what the bushman told, while raging rains
Whirled tempests round our hut at Stockyard Flat,—
Just what he told that night—the self-same tale,
Yet not the self-same words—I tell to-day.
I change his rough to smooth, and simply touch
His bare blunt speech with certain chimes of verse.)

——o——

Hedge round the fire (he said) and while yon blasts
Blow out their gusty summons, friends, give heed!
I speak of griefs and perils, felt and faced
While station-hunting on the Warrego

    *   *   *   *   *   *

Two Seasons had been parched, sirs, and a third
Flamed, droughtier than its fellows, till the grass,
The green, lush grass, grew spoilt by baneful days
And nights that came uncoupled with cool dews.
    And musing much on decimated flocks,
And gaunt herds thinned by dearth of sustenance,

Paul cried, one day, to Oscar ·　" Are we men ?
" Ay, men, I say, or marble?　Plagues and droughts
" Smite the sick land with horrors,—yet we stand
" Slave-like, and smile at buffets !　Comrade, rouse !
" And, ere some wide-mouthed Ruin swallow all,
" Let's seek, far West, some richer pasturing ground !

　　　*　　　*　　　*　　　*　　　*　　　*

So—spurred by strong compulsive need—they went.

　　　*　　　*　　　*　　　*　　　*　　　*

Five days the comrades, journeying horse by horse,
Passed herbless plains, and clay-flats cracked with heat ;
And crossed dry blackened beds, where twisting creeks
And runnels once had brawled.　But loth, (stout hearts !)
To leave that waste with failure in their hands,
They slacked no rein, till, checked by hostile ground,
Their maimed steeds fell,—disabled utterly !

Now, mid those sterile tracts unhorsed, and vexed
With leagues of drought and travail, toiled the friends;
Till Oscar, though the brawnier-limbed, laid hands
(Weak, feverish hands) on Paul, and groaned,—" Enough !"
" Slow torpor numbs my strength, and arduous hours
" Seem changes rung on one perpetual pain.
" Were Heaven's pearled gates in sight, I can no more !"

" Nay, nay," said Paul, " take heart !   To-day, I slew
" A sulphur-coloured snake that doubtless slid
" Due west, toward water-shallows !   Courage, friend !'"

Courage ?   The phrase fell, profitless as grief :
Lost, like a stream, sand-swallowed . vain as tears
That waste, in sleep, when sharp dreams dominate
Courage the man possessed, but supple thews
And sinewy limbs, he lacked   And so, perforce,
They camped beside some samphire-covered hills
That reddened with the sunset.

                                   All that night
Strong Fever marshalled hosts of pains, and plagued
The sick man's flesh ; and when next dawn layed out
God's liberal light, Paul strode where lines of scrub
Buttressed with brushwood yellow mounds of sand—
And roughly reared a screen of boughs, to foil
Noon's fiery edge, and shield his anguished friend

Six days Paul watched : slow days that lagged to nights,
And loitered into morns ; and, on the seventh,
When gathering glooms had sucked light's last faint flakes,
And keen white stars crept, palpitatingly,

Amid unfolding skies, the sick man moaned :—
" Comrade!   On, on to safety !   I am doomed,
" Doomed utterly !   Forsake me, Paul, and fly !"

" May God forsake me, if I do !" said Paul ;
" Though Thirst and Famine come, and sweeping storms
" Clamour and brawl, and shake the world's four walls,
" Paul shall not blench or budge !   Here lies my part,
" Whatever be the issue !"

                              But again,
Slowly the faint voice murmured —" Death draws nigh !
" Yea,—knells his certain summons, for my veins
" Burn, and grow sapless as the dead loose leaves
" That clog the forest aisles in bleak July !
" Heed dying lips ! turn Paul !   O turn and fly !"

" Nay, turn and sleep !" Paul answered, " twice accursed
" By Heaven and earth are cowards.   Sleep ! I say,
" May God forsake me, if I faint and fly !"

Thus spoke a brave heart's friendship : yet, once more,
With passionate persistence wailed the voice :—
" Mid prosperous realms, and cities thronged with life,

" Where millions toil and grovel (soul and flesh

" Bond-slaves to Belial and the Hunger-God),

" While Fortune's favourites heap red gold like mire,—

"'There too, again, mud plains that stretch and show

" Illimitable tracts, whose furnaced sands

" Gasp languidly, and mock the day'—Alas,

" These have I paced, a mateless, childless, man ;

" A solitary soul. For me, no wife,

" (When dry Decembers scorched, or Augusts wept

" Their windy way through ranks of rain-black clouds)

" Cheered, like a seraph, Life's vicissitudes

" For me no babes, with glib bewitching speech,

" Lisped the sweet prate that charms the silent sire

" As bird-psalms charm the bard. O Paul, O Paul,

" On me these heaven-gleams glint not, but on you !

" Close-barred from me, God's largess showers on you !

" Spare, spare the guiltless far ones : pause and fly '"

Here first the stout heart faltered , for the thin

Strained voice had struck one master-chord of Life,

Man's vehement love of quiet household joys,

His heartaches for the witching charms of Home :

But Paul, perplexed and tearful, cried, " Forbear,

" Forbear, Heaven frowns when cravens faint and fly '"

Now darkness circled round them like a spell
And Oscar drowsed, while Paul yearned, moodily,
To pierce that vast void Stillness.   Fitful winds,
Like melancholy night-gasps, waxed, and then
Waned noiselessly, and timorous brushbirds wailed
From out the mallee-scrub and salt-bush clumps
That flanked the dun base of the sand-ridge near

      At times, far dolefuller sounds vexed Paul, for, lo,
Sonorous curlews scudded past, with shrieks
And dismal lamentations, wofuller
Than those dread groans which daunt the woodman's heart
When strong north-easters sweep through swamp-oak groves.

      Forlornly shrilled these wasteland cries, while Paul
Sat, hour by hour, and marvelled if God's Hand,
Past the fierce limits of that wild lone land,
Would guide them to a havened peace again.

     So passed the night; that long and desolate night!—
Throned mid its infinite retinues of stars,
It passed, and gradual day, with stealthy strides,
Stalked slowly, broadly, on.

               Now drifts of cloud
Showed dawn's soft roseprints deepening in the east,
And melting mists made visible far hills.

Huge battlemented crags were they, whose fronts
And fractured summits, gapped by ruthless Time,
And scarred by rains and tempests, frowned on Paul
Like Hell's grim cliffs, and rocks unscalable.

Keen anguish pierced his soul, that brave strong soul,
With toils sore spent, and vexing vigils wrung;
And, glancing where his friend supinely lay,
Paul saw the languid eyes grow luminous
With strange mysterious light, and soon, the voice
Spake hollowly.—

(As when, mid cavernous chasms,
Some lost foot-wanderer wails for succouring aid,
Distinct at first, his shrill voice volleying flies,
Till, checked where wide rifts gape, and huge rocks jut,
It wanes and wastes, and echoes hopelessness,
Meanwhile, high up, (a-drowsing mid their flocks)
Dull hinds catch hints of deep sepulchral cries
That surge like death-sighs from a world of graves ·
So thin, so worn, so hollow, ached that voice :—)

" Midway 'twixt dusk and dawn," it wailed, " I heard
" The cry of crested pigeons, wheeling low,
" And thrice the air grew black with clanging wings,
" And hoarse with marsh-fowls' clamors; (Peace ! I know

" When famished spoonbills, shrieking, scent lagoons !)

" Moreover, at that hour when conquered night

" Shrinks, shuddering, from the dawn, cold winds arose

" And breathed soft benedictions, soothing me

" With sounds like babbling brooks; and then, my pangs

" Ceased, for I heard far torrents !   Paul, be urged !

" Strike south, and seek assistance for us both !"

So moaned the dying Oscar.

                              Paul took up

These last weak words, and thus considered them —

          " Cooped here, Man's bones might bleach till Doom's dread
                    trump

" Thundered confusion on all flesh that lives !

" Christian, or Christless, what man treads these wastes ?

" Here, no oases bloom : no springs outgush :

" Some curse mars all, and battles with mankind !"

So muttering, he unslung the water-flask,

And drew, with niggard hand, their daily dole.

(Ah, God! what fierce extremes encompass Life !

Note yon plump Sybarite, whose noons are feasts,

Whose midnights dainty banquets !   Hedged with gold,

He sucks abundance from earth's shores and seas :

He drains the Wine of Life from jewelled cups,
And fattens well for grave-worms !

Different fares
Yon child of pain that treads dry, furnaced tracts !
Above, stretch skies of fire · around him, plains,
Bare, moistureless : beneath him, earth,—his grave !
For him no rich looms ply with curious skill ;
No menials crook and cringe ; no tempting cates
Nor rare wines glisten : at Fate's Sibyl-hands
He plucks Desire, Mistrust, Hope, Fear, and Death !
Ah God ! what fierce extremes encompass Life !)

Now Thirst, that deadly desert-foe, stalked near ;
For, nestling in their flasks, alas, remained
Scarce three days' water for the body's need:
And Paul, though staid, and nowise fooled by dreams,
Sat piecing Oscar's talk.   He knew, right well,
That dying eyes have strength to see and pierce
Those dim, dark, realms which border Death, and knew
That hands, just loosening from the world, may gain
Their firmest, godliest, grasps of things Divine ;
And thus, perturbed and vexed with hopes and fears,
He mused, well-nigh to madness.

Soon he cried,

"Turn, or turn not, Destruction dogs my heels !

" Slow Death confronts, and Famine follows me,

" Till, like some snared wild beast, bound limb and limb,

" I fall—ignobly trapped ?   Nay, better, I say,

"To face my fate with sinews braced and set,

" And make a manlike end !   Ay, nobler far !

" God help us   I must seek these water-springs !"

With that, Paul's heart seemed some whit comforted ;

For wise resolve both sanctifies and saves ,

Nor do the clefts and caves of legioned Hell

Hold souls more surely damned than wavering men

Who, like light leaves mid windy buffetings,

Whirl restlessly, corrupting day by day !

Here, gathering up what strength lay still unspent

In nerve and thew, Paul sought the patch of scrub,

And, hewing down broad boughs of close-leaved box,

Sped straightway back :—" Because," said he, " rough winds

" May rave and fret the self-same hour I go,

" And rains, perchance, may pelt persistently

" That white wan face ; (ah, horrible rains !) and so

" To match these possibilities, my hand

"Must weatherfend the wurley !"

                             This he did

He bound the thick boughs close with bushman's skill,
Till not a gap was left where raging showers
Or gusts might riot.   Over all, he stretched
 Strong bands of cane-grass, plaited cunningly.

By this high noon had passed, and eve's slant sun
With weak and yellowing gleam just topped the west.

Now stayed Paul's hand till dark —for restful night,
In arid regions, makes cool journeying,
While day's bewildering heats baulk man and beast.
He loitered, then, till dusk, and paced the camp,
With faint but kindling hope, in search of stores
For necessary travel

                           As he turned,

The sick man thrilled convulsively, and lo,
Half-rose, stretched forward, clutched the flagon, poured
Their scant supply in Paul's own travelling-flask,
And swooning, reeled and fell.

                         But Paul beheld !

That small sublime deceit Paul saw, unseen ;

Tears sluiced his eyes, while, grasping Oscar's flask,
He ran the liquid back, and scarcely kept
(To tread that trackless wilderness) as much
As, at a gulp, might ridge the smooth, soft, throat
Of some grey-breasted plover parched with thirst.

    Then, striding where the man lay, motionless,
He sobbed :—" If God's grace guide me—O my friend—
" In yon great range may huddle billabongs ;
" If not,—thy mightier need confutes mine own !"

    Therewith, he placed the flask by Oscar,—aye,
And kissed his white wan brows with that strained kiss,
His bloodless brows with that strained passionate kiss,
Which strong men, in a life time moved, kiss once.
And, shouldering back the fringe of leaves, again
He gazed at Oscar, then, heart-agonized,
Crossed the green threshold

                    Thus went Paul his way !

(O sovereign Love ! sublime 'twixt man and maid,—
But Christlike, more august, 'twixt man and man !
O Power that rules broad realms, and clans, and creeds,
And makes the world's heart jubilant !   O Love,
Majestic Love,—Man's noblest attribute,—
In poor or rich, how beautiful art thou ?

In hind or king how comely?   Yea, from Him
(The sinless, slain, miraculous Nazarene)
Whose red blood ransomed Man, to yon sad wretch
Who, scorned and squalid, starved and desolate,
Feels, yet, compassionate pangs,—most beautiful !
O pure, O mystic Love, that thrives and spreads
Like some strange Tree, whose far roots wrap Man's soul ;
On whose vast boughs crowned Seraphs sit ; whose top
Thrones the veiled splendors of Omnipotence !—
How wonderful art thou !   How wonderful !)

Through night's long hours Paul trod that hopeless land,
Nor neared the peaks till dawn.   Grim hills were they
Whose huge piled blocks seemed poised by giant hands
In high perpetual menace of mankind !

    Athwart their base rough gorges stretched, and past
Precipitous steeps, one large dry gum-creek, paved
With smooth round boulders, and worn gravel-stones.
Its banks were loose and blistered.   Noon's strong heats
Had sucked the stream that once hummed hereabout
True desert-music.   So Paul drooped, forlorn,
(Prone on a sandstone block) with head that bent
As bends some battered bulrush, maimed by rains,
And sapped by sudden storms

But what boots Grief
When Life craves action ?   Therefore Paul arose,
And searched those stubborn sands with hot, keen, eyes,
For some small glimpse of help.

At length he scanned
A faint old sheep-trail, trending northwardly :—
And, as a cave-lost man, mid murk and gloom,
Grows wild with hope, and hails some distant gleam,
So Paul exulted there !   With frenzied eyes,
That often lost, but swiftlier found, the tracks,
And feet that faltered rarely, on he pressed,
Till daylight waxed and waned, and dusk warned " *Hold.*"

With night came coupled Dread.

For merciless thirst
Nipt the worn wanderer, till he drained the flask,
And hurled the shell afar.   Then Sleep,—soft Sleep,—
Kind, pitiful, Sleep—crept drowsily, and wrapt
The tough, racked, body in dreamless rest.

Next morn,
Fierce rose the sun, and smote him,—smote him, Sirs,—
Till pains and throbbings roused him.   Whereupon,
Upgathering to his feet, he searched anew.

By noon, the sandwaste altered,—for the ground
Grew strewn with splintered, flint-like, stones that took
A dull and tawny hue, i' the strong sun's glare.

      To plod long leagues of sand seemed hard; but now,
More terrible toils were Paul's. His wayworn feet
Fared bitterly on sharp, unstable flints,
And slipped and stumbled, till by prints of blood
His limping way was landmarked. Still, brave heart,
His strong will urged him onward; for he deemed
The flints might form that girdling stony zone,
Which oft, in sterile regions, belts the plain,
(Sand-flanked on either side.) He, therefore, aimed
To cross that strip with speed, and haply reach
More promising plains beyond.

          But Hope unhelped
Soon famishes Man's flesh,—and, when Fatigue
Strangled the Trust that homed within his heart
Like some supernal guardian, Paul's faint strength
Waned with the westering sun, whose nether rim,
Low-poised, and luminous, reddened on the verge
Of sands far reaching westward. As it sank,
Prone, on the plain, he swooned without a cry,
And lay, outstretched, till dawn.

      Throughout that night,
Cool dews came sallying on that rain-starved land,
And drenched the thick rough tufts of bristly grass
Which, stemmed like quills, (and thence termed porcupine)
Thrust, hardily, thin shoots amid the flints
And sharp-edged stones

     Soon, fan-shaped, spread the dawn ·
And, kinglike, pranked with pomps of ushering clouds,
The crimson cruel sun arose, and trailed
Swift through that sterile plain red skirts of fire !
Hell's grip was on his heart again !—Paul stirred—
Cried muttered cries, and woke right wearily.
  And seeing those coarse stalks diamonded with dew,
Yea, webbed and wet with beaded filaments,
He grovelled low, and scooped his black burnt mouth,
To suck the dwindling drops, whereat, in truth,
One small wood-swallow scarce could sip.

     Driven wild,
And desperate in his life's supremest need,
Once more he staggered on.

     And now the sun
Climbed to the topmost heaven, and steadfastly

Shone with consuming strength, until the air
Glowed like a thing incorporate with the flames
That scorched and stung Paul's brain. I tell you, Sirs,
Through all earth's myriad tribes, God saw that day
No mournfuller sight than he! At length, alas,
Both plain and sky seemed suddenly to swirl
And plunge down dreamless deeps where Famine, Thirst,
And Anguish sank from sight,—far underworlds
Where Death and Silence reigned Lords Paramount.

　　　Even that swoon passed , for life was strong —and then
Trooped dead delights which perished days had known !
For dreamscapes came and went of years when life
Was like some scroll, fast-shut, of wizard-lore
Mysterious and unknown　In dim vague dreams,
He roamed, once more, through haunts of innocent youth.
He saw Monaro's peaks whose kingly crests
Bulk skyward from the vales to glance at God —
Hills robed in light, august, majestical,—
And fruitful vales, whose breadths of delicate green
Are dear to nibbling flocks, and herds that browse.
　　　In visioned vista, too, its broad rich plains
And loamy meadows stretched,—and, chiefliest, one
(By Love, that subtle sleuth-hound, tracked) wherein

His father's homestead stood, like some fair Ark
Mid seas of billowing grain.

                                        Beguiled, he wept.

Anon, with Sleep and Memory, strode his sire, —
A gracious man, grave-browed with Care, and crowned
With meditative Age's concomitant,
Experience ripely-garnered.   By his side,
Girt with serenest grace, the mother gazed
Regardfully   Her eyes (two mournful moons)
Made glorious with the lovelight shrined in them,
Blabbed tenderly from fond clear depths life's first
Unfathomable boon,—maternal love —
That old perennial spell which still outcharms
The spurious lesser loves that fret mankind.

Again came mortal pangs.

                        Home's golden dreams
And pageants bulked once more to things of dread
That nightmared Paul.   Myriads of monstrous hands,
Gaunt, claw-tipped, seemed to writhe from out fierce skies,
   And pluck him back to life and agony,—
At which, with terrible cries, the swooner woke.

He lay upon the plain, with limbs diffused ;—
Half-tombed by drifting sands. One down-stretched hand
Had delved a hollowed place some four spans deep,
Athirst, perchance, to grasp beneath parched plains,
Coolness, denied above.   Or, haply else,
As though the soul's continual aches had warned
The weak, faint frame to scoop its grassless grave
Past reach of kites and prowling warrigals.

'His bare right arm was flesh-torn to the bone,
As if by wild beasts' teeth ; and, on the wounds
Swarmed crawling crowds of small black ants, that cleansed
The thick and oozing blood-clots.   Aye, amid
Delirious hours, self-lacerating teeth
Had gnawed Paul's own shrunk limb, and famished lips
Had fastened on impoverished veins, and drained
The oil that fuelled life's spasmodic flame
(Though wrought in madness, this was horrible!)
And, weakening fast, Paul feebly cloaked his face,
And waited for the end !

He felt that soon
His white and graveless bones would front the sun
In gleaming accusation of day's wrath.
That soon his dust would whirl unsepulchred,
Nor requiemed, save by wails from those quick winds

That sink and swell about the night's mid-heart.
And, crushed by stress of suffering, he played
The hand of Death—of dumb relentless Death—
Might free his soul

             Even thus the Enemy neared
A ravenous Presence,—vague, intangible,—
That blindly sucked his life   Its clammy breath
(Like dews that reek and drip from charnel vaults)
Froze anguish into stupor; and sharp films
Bleared his faint, heavy, eyelids as he gasped—
     " Mother,—farewell,—farewell,—wife,—children,"—

     *   *   *   *   *   *

                              " Hold!
" Quick—quick—my man! just tilt that water flask!
" Leftwards.—now drench him!—So· he's coming-to!"
And Paul strained up,—beheld strong, bearded men,
Heard helpful words, and swooned to nothingness!

     *   *   *   *   *   *

Of Oscar? Friends, I kept my tale's straight march,
And so spared speech of Oscar. Yet, when Paul
Plucked, from a three-months' fever, what remained
Of pristine health and strength,—he told, at large,
Of desperate perils, faced where seldom rain

Cheers the baked earth —told, too, of wastelands strewn
With keen-edged shards, and fragmentary flints,
Till rude, rough, bush-hands wept compassionate tears.

    Ranging, he spoke of Oscar ; hunger-clung
Beneath that bough-piled gunyah   But, at this,
The plain, rough, listeners shook half-doubtful heads,
And shrugged incredulous shoulder-shrugs, and saying,—
" Wild Fever's seeds yet linger in the man !"
Put forth no hand of help

                  Yet, sirs, they lie,
Who say Paul closed with such cold counsellings
I say they lie !   Through hazardous months of pain,
Paul sought his comrade's death-place night and day—
But where those naked bones blanch, God, who knows,
Has kept from friend and kin.

               SIRS, I AM PAUL !

Abrupt, he ceased ·—and grave thoughts chained us all,
Till Reed cried, " Boys ! bestir ! the tempest's past !"
Whereat, each slipped to saddle, and was gone.

So ran that tale of risks and jeopardies
Which menace man amid our inland wilds .—

And though Regret feigns hopefuller things, and sighs
" 'Twas well with Oscar's soul," I know (alas !)
Earth's banefullest pains and plagues rain thick on men
That waste amid untravelled tracts, consumed
By pestilent Thirst, and past-cure maladies.

From which dire straits protect us, O our Lord,
Who perished crosswise on the Tree Accursed !

The Garland—To Charlotte.

Accept, my Queen, the garland I present,
  And note the moral masked in its selection ,
For jewel-colored flowers, in beauty blent,
    Meet here to form perfection !

Choice growths, I say, of many a bud that blows
  I group with floral skill, that I may render
The bright, pure, chaplet which my hands compose,
    One of surpassing splendor

And, viewing the contrasted tints herein,
  My nimble brain, with wayward humour, traces
Fine, subtle, hints that quaintly seem akin
    To thy peculiar graces.

For as, past doubt, each blossom here entwined,
  Hangs somewhat on its neighbouring buds dependent,
And only when with different hues combined
    Proves perfectly resplendent,—

So lives and blooms in thine imperial soul
 The fragrant flower of every charming duty,
Whose gracious union makes the faultless whole
  Which crowns thy life with beauty!

Yea, guards thine heart (that shrine supremely fair!)
 With templed thoughts that turn from Sin's aggression,
For each desire, my Queen, which nestles there,
  Is Virtue's chaste possession.

Hagar and Ishmael.

(A Scriptural Paraphrase.)

Where the wastes of Beersheba stretch, sweltering and bare,
And the swart Arab shrinks from Day's merciless splendor
That strikes like a plague, through the pendulous air,
   Scorching growths, green and tender ;—
Even there, past rough deserts, the scorned Hagar came,
With a desolate heart, and faint, travel-spent frame,
Leading Ishmael, the child of her love and her shame

Gaunt hills, and weird pinnacles, gloomed through the sands
Of that perilous realm, to perplex and confound her ;—
Strange horrors that hiddenly compass lone lands
   Thronged in legions around her,—
Till she moaned ·—" Ere I swoon mid this limitless wild,
" Let my desperate steps track some spring undefiled,
" To soothe thy burnt brows, and parched limbs, O my child ! "

" Ah, Ishmael ! spurned son ' when the love of thee crept
" To my granite-walled heart, Life's glad sun seemed new-risen ;

" My soul laughed and leapt, which, till then, dumbly slept
  " In my body's base prison;—
" Aye, and now, though huge Frenzy gripe hard to prevail,
" Love nerves strengthless limbs, prone to falter and fail,
" And a heart fain to break in one agonised wail ! "

So moaning, she stumbled on, tortured by flints,
Over rocky defiles, and harsh sand-gaps and hollows,
Thirst's fantasies mock her with fraudulent hints,
  Which her jaded foot follows :—
But the strong sun had scoured the dry, shelterless, plain,
Till each moist nook, that once stored the delicate rain,
Clean-emptied, could bless neither lip nor hot brain '

Still the skies throbbed,—pulsating fierce flames—till, at length,
Stalked Despair, with a visage relentless and cruel,
And snatched from the outcast that scantling of strength
  To which Hope had been fuel
And, shrouding the child from high Noon's baleful glare,
She groaned to the shut skies this ultimate prayer.—
" Die, Ishmael ; yet God keep my soul unaware ! "

" *What aileth thee, Hagar ?* "   (She cowers to the sod ')
See ! Heaven's manifold mercy cleaves dense air in sunder :

And the bondwoman's heart bounds exulting to God
   In a spasm of mute wonder .—
" *Rise, Hagar ! with Ishmael, thy life's sweet delight !* "
Then, bewildered, she turned, where miraculous, bright,
Crisp, runnels brawled, babbling of Help in her sight

L'ENVOI.

Even so, when Grief buffets thy vexed heart about,
Till, bruised by disasters, Life's temple seem shaken,—
O friend, be well-counselled, lest, haply, thou doubt,
   And tall,—wholly forsaken.
For though God, Whose great Hand holds mortality's dust,
With the same sun greet chaste souls, and vassals of lust,
Aye, though earth's treasures teem for both just and unjust,
I know He rains blessings on Patience and Trust.

Sonnet

SLEEP AND FAME.

Supinely stretched, with eyes that ached to drowse,
Last noon I nestled from the sun's strong flame,
Perplexed and pained, till timorous Sleep became
A tranquil prisoner in my tremulous brows.

    Then those swift, wayward, sprites that nimbly rouse
When easeful Morpheus clasps Man's bodily frame,
Beset my slumbrous sense, and harped on Fame!
    And one sprite said.—"O thou of rhythmic vows!
" Whose sounding songs make music in our ears!
" Choose Life's ephemeral laud, or *future* bays,—
" Since whoso reaps a splendid present praise,
" Shall lack continuance in more distant years!"

    I heard —but ere my slow speech, stumbling, said,
" *Choose me the latter!* "—lo! the visioned couriers fled!

Sonnet

TO MY MOTHER.

Compulsive Force, which rules Man's temporal fate,
May clutch my fond home-yearnings by the throat,
And, deaf to clamorous wail, and wild debate,
May turn my face toward perilous climes, remote!

Fair, alien, realms athwart mine eyes may float,
And tracts (alas!) more venomous than Hate!
And flowerful heaths, where honeyed bees might gloat
From diamond-morn, till night creeps, starred with state!

My frame, sun-scorched, may press through treeless sands·
Or shrink, transfixed by churlish snows that smite,—
Yea,—though I traverse Earth's most radiant lands,
And share their sumptuous hoards of rich delight,—

No charm, or change, sweet Mother, that sense may see
Shall tempt my allegiance, once, from memories born of thee!

The Crown of Life.

Some seek divine Content mid sylvan glades—
And, lo, where woodland shades
(Made bright with green things beautiful) beseech
Man's rapt, responsive speech—
Embayed and fenced from baffling greed and gain,
Strive, with uneager passion, to attain
Those mild immunities from jarring strife
Which wed soft Peace to Life.

Some yearn, within the brisk Town's jangling marts,
To sate their covetous hearts!—
They scheme shrewd plots—aye, unabashed, and bold,
Cheat,—hungry-mouthed for gold!
And some deem fair a calm luxurious vale,
Wherein their souls might sumptuously inhale
Scents, blown by drifts from paradisal groves
What time bland zephyr roves.

Some, poised upon the rough Deep's wind-driven foam,
Disdain the lures of home.

To them, sharp rocks, and shallows of the sea
Seem themes of jest and glee—'
For wayward waves hold some transcendent charm
By which they hope to prosper, freed from harm,
When storms, that sweep great ships to gulfy graves,
Thunder through Ocean's caves

Some, (thralled by Vice) mid light voluptuous ways,
Would waste Life's few brief days
O, hearts unwise! beneath your cozening wine
Coiled asps, perchance, entwine!
And, lo, when sensuous Beauty buds in smiles,
Or speaks bewitching words, Love's snares and wiles
Vex, with besieging sorrows, Man's delight,
And haunt him, day and night

To some,—high peaks, whose haughty summits rise
As though they cleft the skies,
Are gladsome,—for they leave the grovelling sod,
For loftier realms, near God
Sweet, too, are odorous dells, where each tired sense
Can revel in delicious indolence,—
And sweet are sunlit slopes, whose flowerful nooks
Are brightly interveined with babbling brooks.

Behold, these varying boons, and myriads more
Men, day by day, implore !
O visionary dreams !—Heaven's gift—*Content*—
Crowns days and years well spent ·—
And appertains, alone, to that grand soul
Whose strenuous strength can pierce beyond Death's goal,
And see, with gathering Hope, past earth's blank sod,
Those mystic quietudes which stream from God !

John Dunmore Lang.

Four years have rolled since, crowned with age and glory,
  You slept Death's sleep, and passed with scarce one sigh,
And gained, by acts that gleam through Austral story,
        A fame that shall not die.

Four years have flown ;—and now, with strong emotion,
  Our grateful land proclaims its boundless debt,
Recalls your patriot-deeds, and life's devotion,
        And mourns, with keen regret.

A brave, great soul was yours ! In sturdiest fashion
  You scorned the stroke of Fate's most adverse dart,
Yet bore within your breast a large compassion,
        And flower-soft, woman's heart.

Ah, with what strenuous strength, in days long perished,
  You toiled and fought for just and righteous laws ;—
Smote Force and Fraud, but ever cheered and cherished
        The People's sacred cause.

And, day by day, and year by year, uprearing
    Fair Freedom's flag,—you trod bright Honour's track;
Pale dastards shrank before you,—and, unfearing,
        You drove harsh despots back.

Yea, in dark days, before our land's grand dawning,
    Mid glooms—where-through no shaft of sunrise broke—
Loud rang your voice, till, like triumphant Morning,
        Our Austral realm awoke.

And, far o'er-sea, where hungering millions languished,
    Your trumpet-tongue made known our bounteous stores;
You showed dim drooping eyes and hearts that anguished,
        Elysiums on our shores!

Amazed, men heard! For here, where Desolation,
    Since Time's first dawn, had made its loneliest den,
Sprang life and light; and lo, a nascent nation
        Arose, of freeborn men !

Time tests rare worth:— and now, by Fame recorded,
    Your splendid deeds plead—luminous, though mute;
Your vigils, toils, and strifes, at last rewarded,
        Are rich in noblest fruit.

JOHN DUNMORE LANG.

High, mid our loftiest sons, and greatest sages,
By Wentworth's shade, methinks I see you stand—
The mightiest twain that light our History's pages,
    The monarchs of our land!

Take, then, our love's best offering! Here, we tender
To you,—to all who stood on heights sublime
And smote our Stygian night with Freedom's splendor,—
    Our homage for all time!

L'ENVOI.

Song, till some lordlier gift—made fair and floral—
Some Rose of rhyme—bloom forth from lips august—
Go, take my own scant wreath, and leaf of laurel,
    And place them by his dust!

                 [1882.]

Sonnet

THE ASTRONOMER.

He stands aloof from grovelling souls that strain
With keen desires, and toilings manifold,
To lard their leanness with the graceless gold
That Greed and Avarice wring from human pain !—
The sensuous aims of earth's voluptuous train—
Whose days are days of mirth, whose nights behold
The poisonous stores of sin and sloth outrolled—
Shake not with Passion's pangs his kinglier brain !—
For, at his ardent glance, night's orbed domain
Unbars her marvellous wealth of stars untold,
And hymns the splendors of their mystic mould
With lyric lapse of song and sweet refrain.—
Heedful, he hears,—while, with subdued delight,
He tracks God's soundless steps through labyrinthine night.

Hast Thou Forgotten Me?

Hast thou forgotten me? the days are dark ;—
Light ebbs from Heaven, and songless soars the lark—
Vexed like my heart, loud moans the unquiet sea—
      Hast thou forgotten me?

Hast thou forgotten me?   O dead delight
Whose dreams and memories torture me to-night—
O love—my life!   O sweet—so fair to see—
      Hast thou forgotten me?

Hast thou forgotten?   Lo, if one should say—
Noontide were night, or night were flaming day—
Grief blinds mine eyes, I know not which it be !
      Hast thou forgotten me?

Hast thou forgotten?   Ah, if Death should come—
Close my sad eyes, and charm my song-bird dumb—
Tired of strange woes—my fate were hailed with glee—
      Hast thou forgotten me?

Hast thou forgotten me?   What joy have I?
A dim blown bird beneath an alien sky,—
O that on mighty pinions I could flee—
          Hast thou forgotten me ?

Hast thou forgotten ?   Yea, Love's horoscope
Is blurred with tears and suffering beyond Hope—
Ah, like dead leaves forsaken of the tree,
          Thou hast forgotten me.

Ireland in the Famine Year, (1880.)

" What voice is this, which, wailing past the waters,
Rolls dirge on dirge of anguish in our ears ?
What Rachel mourns, anew, for sons and daughters ?
    Mourns, with a mother's tears ?

" Joy's beams once brightened round her ; but, thereafter,
Grief whirled strange blasts, and now sharp woes have come ;
What ails your ancient mirth, O lips of laughter ?
    What smites your music dumb ?

" Sobs mar, indeed, your face where beauties blended,
Sighs shake your voice of Song, and, in your eyes,
Tears blot that brilliant light, once soft and splendid
    As Heaven's own faultless skies

" Of old, your jovial jests made glad the nations ;
Wit's radiant self hung raptured on your lips —
Who wrenched your lyric mouth with lamentations ?
    What clothed you with eclipse ? "

Sad ERIN hears my words; and, weeping faster,
Tells—while deep sighs pant quivering on her tongue—
How, leagued with Want, and deadly with Disaster,
    Gaunt Famine blights her young.

Nor yet, alone, her young '—old man and maiden,
Child, parent, all, breathe out one hopeless breath;
Her plague-struck air rolls melancholy, laden
    With fumes and seeds of death

Even thus she pleads, with agonized emotion;
Pleads for dear lives fast dwindling to the grave;
Yearns with strong prayers, and craves across the ocean
    The bounty that shall save

Ah! shall she fail?   See, Britons, in your annals,
When Valour's van sustained rough Battle's shock,
How Erin's sons strode first through War's red channels,
    Firm, steadfast as a rock

With you, they crushed your foes; and, mid War's thunder,
When Strife's wild flag through sanguine fields unfurled,
Your charge, combined, o'erwhelmed and clove in sunder
    The warriors of the world.

Repay these patriot-debts! Now, panged with sorrow,
By Famine hedged—and pale, with suppliant hands,
Grieved for To-day, and desperate for To-morrow,
    Before you ERIN stands.

Help, then, for Christ's sweet sake!—O souls made earnest
By Faith, by Hope, by love for anguished Man —
Join hands, and bid this plague, so fierce and furnaced
    End—swift as it began!

France in 1870.

(THE YEAR OF THE TRIUMPH OF GERMANY.)

Blown past five thousand leagues of foam, the wild war-clamor
    comes,—

I hear the tramp of hurrying troops, the brattling peals of drums,—

At cries that rise, like agonies, my sorrowing soul is mute,—

        For round each plain,

        Where Strife holds reign,

The Tree of Carnage thrives amain, and Death plucks red, ripe, fruit.

Like fiends let loose from Hell's black pits, War's tempest-terrors
    whelm,—

Till, shattered by a thousand shocks, France sinks her splintered
    helm.

The strongest of her stalwart sons are writhing on the sod,—

        And, from the slain,

        (Past reach of pain)

Freed souls arise, mid crimson rain, not unavenged, to God!

The tranquil slopes of rich Lorraine, the happy vales of Rhine,
Are splashed and blurred with ruddier streaks than purple spilth
    of wine;—
Some sun-browned tillers of the soil lie stark in Rhenish lands,
              And others, vain
              Of slaughter's stain,
Live,—branded by the ban of Cain,—with homicidal hands!

God's great curse grapple with the knaves who, spurred by venomed
    ire,
Cry " *Havoc*," till men's hearts become red wastes of ruin-fire.
God's malison consume them, be they despots, kings, or clowns,
            Whose quarrels chain
            Each quivering vein,
Till famished vultures reap the gain when chieftains brawl for
    Crowns!

Ah! tears fall fast round desolate hearths! Sad lips sigh many a
    moan—
Sigh many a prayer that pleads—" O Death! we live unloved and
    lone!
" Draw near, O grave, and fold us in your deep, unvexed, repose!"
            For bitter pain,
            And anguish, wane
And shrink from the unconscious brain at Life's lethargic close!

O Peace, thou timorous fugitive ;—white-robed in saintliest stole—
Glide graciously where wailing souls lament at War's harsh goal—
Uproot, expel, the bitter feuds that sever hearts from hearts—

    And re-ordain

    That grape and grain

Shall shine through Rhineland's meadowy plain, and bless her
    straitened marts !

Man's mortal term, supernal Maid, falls perilous and brief !
Scant hopes, and measureless despairs fulfil his years of grief—
Quench, then, his thirst for turbulence, and bid his hate desist,

    Till King and Swain,

    From strife refrain,

And mutual Love, alone, remain Earth's glad monopolist !

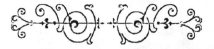

A Love Lyric.

To shun each haunt of mocking mirth,
And lightly look on human kind ·—
To shrine thy form of marvellous worth,
As guardian of my moveless mind ;—
To hear thy voice in singing streams,
Or in the torrent's thunderous roar,
To view thee in my nightly dreams,
And, waking, muse on thee the more —
    Can this be Love ?

To trace thee in untrampled sands,
Or in the vast and billowy sea ;
To find that earth's far-regioned lands
Abate, no jot, my griefs for thee ·—
To cry aloud, " *O sluggish sun,*
Bestir thy steeds, and urge the night,—"
And yet, ere shadowy eve be done,
To yearn, again, for blithesome light —
    Can this be Love ?

To haunt the trackless woodland-maze,
And deem that whispering leaves avow
The beauty of thy tranquil ways
In murmurings from each wind-tossed bough ,

To hear glad birds in twittering throngs
Trill happy strains from raptured throats,
And yet account their witching songs
Harsh discords to thine own sweet notes :—
Can this be Love?

To think of thee in that charmed hour
When bland, soft, airs vacate their caves ;
Or when sharp storms, with tyrant power,
Despoil strong earth, and rule the waves.
Or mid the faint and slumbrous plash
Of surges in enchanted sleep ;
Or when, with stern, relentless dash,
The big seas vex the whitening Deep ·—
Can this be Love?

To gaze at night's transcendent eyes
While passionate thought my soul absorbs ;
To waft divine, delicious, sighs
Amid those sad mysterious orbs :—
To find perpetual hints of thee,
In earth, and sky, and sea, and air,
And feel that, distant though I flee,
Thine image greets me everywhere :—
Yes! this is Love!

Death and Dives.

(A SCRIPTURAL PARAPHRASE.)

"*And he said, 'This will I do'*   *   *   *   *But God said unto him,*
thou fool, this night thy soul shall be required of thee."—LUKE.

DIVES:—Now my manifold toilings have ceased, I am blithesome
and bold!

    For life's rigour abates,

  And my spirit grows rapturous, fired with the gleam of
my gold!

DEATH —*Lo! yon fool idly prates!*

DIVES —I will build mighty garners for grain   both my cattle
and wheat

    Shall astonish mankind!—

  All the lank knaves that Penury breeds shall be dust to
my feet!

DEATH —*Fool! madman, and blind!*

DIVES :—I will rear sumptuous mansions, and waft mid rich tapestried rooms

Subtle odors unseen,—

Till my passionate sense swoon, bewitched with soft fragrant perfumes :—

DEATH —*A fool's Eden I ween !*

DIVES :—I will pillage proud realms for far dainties !—the spoils of the sea,

And the gifts of each land—

Quick slaves, nimbler-footed than tempests, shall gather for me !— ,

DEATH :—*Shall this weaken mine hand ?*

DIVES :—As I banquet, youths wondrous in music with harps shall advance

Chanting songs quaint and rare !

While sweet-singing damsels delectably whirl through the dance !

DEATH :—*I too, may be there !*

DIVES :—I will search out voluptuous pursuits for each fleet hour that glides,

Till my charmed soul affirm

Her felicity buttressed and built like an oak that abides !

DEATH :—*Till abased by a worm !*

DIVES:—I will gloat amid measureless pleasures, and surfeit with
glee.—

And mankind shall exclaim—

"Were the world one wide kingdom of laughter, its
Monarch were he!"

DEATH —*Slave,—rather,—of Shame!*

DIVES —O my soul! as a bound sheaf mid sheaves be thou folded
in bliss:

Yea,—exult at thy lot!—

Happy days that hereafter transpire, be ye echoes of this!

DEATH :—*Now, the fool's bolt is shot!*

DIVES·—Ah! from sun-rise to star-rise, from dusk till night wastes
at day's door,

Reign,—lapped in delight!

Let to-morrow shine out like to-day, but abundantly more!

DEATH —*Fool! perish this night!*

DIVES :—Sleep! soothe me awhile, for a strange pang, with violent
touch,

Thrilled my body outright.—

Peradventure, O soul, with keen joys thou art tired over-
much!

DEATH :—*Fool! perish this night!*

DIVES.—Woe's me! like a sword that drives deep past the joints
  of the mail,
    When mailed warriors fight.—
      Bitter agonies swim through my sinews,—I falter,—I fail!
DEATH.—*Fool! perish this night!*

DIVES.—As a spoken speech ebbs from man's lips —yea, as leaves
  eddy by
    When rough winter-gusts rave,—
      Even so,—foully wrenched from Life's splendors,—ah,—
        help,—God—*I die'*
DEATH :—*Thou art Conqueror,—O Grave'*

Song.

LOTH TO DEPART.

Loth to depart! long I sighed for that sight of you
Smitten, transfixed, by the subtle god's dart,—
Then I turned homeward,—and, dreaming all night of you,
Slept, with a limitless joy round my heart.
Soft were your vows, but the Hope that pulsed strong in them
Swift through my soul Love's own lava-tide rolled :—
Brief were your words, but the chime of the song in them
Charmed like the chant of the syrens of old !

Loth to depart ! ah, that glimpse—ah, that gleam of you
Clung to me, cheered me, bewitched me, and stayed,—
Made of each day but one exquisite dream of you
Hallowed each night as with mystical aid —
Loth —yet I went!—and, for years that were drear to me—
Years of harsh vigils and infinite toils—
Fought with my Fate for the girl that was dear to me—
Grappled with Fortune,—and conquered the spoils !

Loth to depart! yet what bliss was Return to me?
Love sprang transfigured as Hope gleamed in sight,—
- Happiness bloomed—and the paths that were stern to me
Broke into beauty,—and blossomed with light!
Now, like the bell-birds, whose magical notes to us
Ring by yon stream till it ripples with song—
Sweet,—let the years of the Future that floats to us
Ripple with melody—all our lives long!

Love's Lamentation.

"Set me as a seal upon thine heart, * * * Many waters cannot quench
Love, neither can the floods drown it."—SOLOMON'S SONG.

O steadfast Love!—more strong than sea-girt rocks
    Round which the rough surge laves ;—
That stand, triumphant, mid the mightiest shocks
    Of warring winds or waves,—
O powerful Love!—majestic as the star
    That governs Day's bright skies,
And showers God's boon of prodigal light afar
    On hungering eyes!

Thou art not symbolized by any flower
    Or gem that man has prized :—
Thine own perennial splendors make thy power
    (O Love) immortalized!
Thou art not emblemed by the wide wild sea
    That belts rich earth around!
What deeps or gulfs, O Love, can image thee ?
    What shores can bound?

My bliss, and bane ! When last I paced yon strand,—
    Glad, with assured delight,
I saw my love's light shallop leave the land
    And, seaward, wing its flight!—

The great round sun loomed low ;—bedraped and pranked
    With black fantastic clouds,
And ah ! the tremulous sky grew crossed and flanked
    With mists like shrouds.

Day drooped his plumes of gold :—hoarse fiends of air
    Sprang up with clamorous mirth,
Loosed the red whirlwinds from their thunder-lair,
    And ravaged sea and earth :—
Fear's palsying films my dim, strained, sight bedewed,
    (Higher the bleak brine surged !)
For in the storm's blind march, Love's sail I viewed,
    Wind-driven, sea-scourged !

Than quick chaff, winnowed by the whirl-blast's hand,
    Swifter the shallop's pace :—
I saw the frail blown boat draw near the land :—
    (Near, till I saw *his* face !)
The wild, wild, waves raged, foaming out their strife,
    And shrill blasts drowned his moan,—
O lost, lost, Love ! Hell's malice crushed thy life,—
    And marred mine own !

Ay me ! cold-cradled in thine oozy home,
    Thou grim, pernicious Deep,—
Mid cerements of the grave, white-fringed with foam,
    My perished love found sleep.
Thy rage set free his soul from joys and cares,—
    One touch bade all surcease—

Barred out Life's raptured hopes, and bleak despairs,
   And brought him Peace.

*   *   *   *   *   *

All night the storm-winds slackened not, but wailed
   Their dirge of undelight :—
The surge, all night, spat flakes of froth, and railed,
   Mocking my passionate plight :—
All night the rain sobbed strange weird monotones,
   And pounced with furious spite,—
As, from my shuddering soul, Hope ebbed in moans—
   In moans,—all night !

*   *   *   *   *   *

Dull eve limps heavily, as maimed with pain,—
   And hark, with pattering feet,
The night creeps, trammelled with the trampling rain,
   And thick with plunging sleet ;—
Days dawn and die :—foul nights and fair depart,
   Nor intermit Grief's song ·
While, like a battered bird, with bleeding heart,
   I linger, O Death, how long ?

A Dream Within a Dream.

"Sweet Sleep, bar out Life's grovelling schemes and themes,"—
  (I said) ; and soon, mid dreams,
I stood, at night, by shores of slumbrous seas
  That slept in death-like ease ;
Whose shimmering sands, more white than thrice-blanched snow,
Mocked the moon's splendor with their spectral glow.

Her disc, round-orbed, shot rays aslant the Deep
  That lay transfixed by sleep.
The waveless waste like luminous silver glowed
  Yet it nor ebbed nor flowed,—
But seemed like one who, wearied past complaining,
Supinely stretched, had yielded to enchaining.

Its shores were girt with immemorial oaks
  Scarred by no rude axe-strokes,—
And far remote, yet seen by subtle sights,
  Mysterious snow-capt heights
Thrust up pale gleaming peaks 'twixt earth and sky.
(No stronger glamour yet charmed dreaming eye !)

I saw a strange thin mist forsake the seas,
   And glide by slow degrees,
Till, at a bow-shot backward from the shore,
   The cloud advanced no more ;—
But swirled in spiral wreaths, and strangely strove
For leafy lodgment in that ancient grove

And soon the mist, pulsating as with life,
   Won in the soundless strife,—
Till bird-like, on the trees' umbrageous breast,
   It swooned to pallid rest.—
And where the topmost branches twined and kissed,
The moon's calm splendors diademed the mist.

But now, athwart the moon, the vaporous cloud
   Rolled upward like a shroud,—
And timorous winds that shunned the bright keen light
   Took heart, and spake outright,—
And quick rough gusts flew ominously past
Like petrels of the fierce tempestuous blast

The gusts ran rumouring with the sluggish waves,—
   And claimed them bounden slaves,—
But they, incensed at being roused so soon
   From Lethargy's dull swoon—
With blustering looks, and ruffled crest replied,
And all allegiance turbulently denied.

Now ceased the spell!—the waves' enchanted way
  Grew chequered with blown spray!—
The mystic cloud returned: and, by degrees,
  Sank in the heaving seas,—
And lo, like one by vague portents dismayed,
I sought, with stumbling feet, the forest shade

High up, like funeral plumes that deck the dead,
Titanic oaks swayed, groaning overhead,—
Yet aimlessly I wandered,—till I found
A noiseless nook amid this haunted ground—
Where, canopied with flowers, and crowned with ease,
Serene delights through all my spirit crept,
And lulled by amorous murmurings of the trees
Sleep's happy languors soothed me, and I slept.

II.

For three long hours mild Sleep's supreme content
  With no harsh dream seemed blent.—
Dim shadowy shapes then, nimbly hovering near,
  Hummed faintly in mine ear:—
With plumy wooing wings awhile they fanned
  My brows on either hand,—
And rained bewildering scents around, and sought
  To sadden me with thought.

But one swift sprite, on powerful pinions, sped
  Hard by my arborous bed,—

Breathed on mine eyes, and sang, " Dull eyes unclose ! "
  " O sleeper, shun repose ! "

Thereat, with tender touch, he purged my sight,-
  Till I, beholding right,
Knew well the white-winged shape that pressed the sod :
  (It was the young Love-god !)
And glancing upward, with dilated eyes,
  (Where nestled dumb Surprise !)
My troubled spirit marvelled much to find
  The beauteous Boy-god blind.
Eager to know whose vengeful hand had thrust
  Love's beauty in the dust—
My loyal lips, for very Sorrow's sake,
  Took Pity's tones, and spake :—

" O god multipotent, whose glad sad sway
  " Dates from Man's earliest day ;—
" Whose world-wide power shall seminate and spread
  " Till earth, itself, be dead :-
" Reveal to me if thou, by fraud betrayed,
  " Wast plunged in sightless shade,—
" Or whether Heaven, so prodigal beside,
  " Light, from the first, denied."—

I ceased —for quick Grief sluiced mine eyes amain,
  And tear-drops fell like rain.

Then mourned the boy of Jove's imperial guile,
And tuned his dulcet voice to song the while,—
Grand as a harp's august, harmonic, swell,—
Yet sweet as strains that vibrate through a shell :—

"Ah, finite-minded man!" (full soft he sighs!)
"Thy matchless maid hath stolen mine heaven-born eyes!
"Jove framed her form supreme in peerless grace,
"And filched mine orbs to gem her glorious face;
"Nor canst thou sorrow—since, by His decree,
"They beam, (well-pleased, I heard!) "*and beam for thee!*"

He spoke:—and lo, responsive to his plaint,
    The pitying winds waxed faint,—
Each blossom, blown and budding, hung its head,
As though by stress of sympathy struck dead —

While thus I lay,—with drowsy joys beguiled,
    Methought the cherub-child
Extended glittering wings, and straightway flew
    Beyond my strenuous view,—
For slumber then withdrew her facile yoke,
And, disenthralled from dreams, *doubly I woke.*

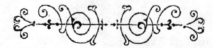

Sonnet

THE HOUSE OF MOURNING.

"The heart of the wise is in the House of Mourning —but the heart of fools is in the House of Mirth "—ECCLESIASTES.

Make mouths :—laugh out Life's span :—O ribald wits !
The smallest straws are midwives to your laughter !
Fling gibes and jests while slippery Time permits,
As if no swallowing Grave gaped wide hereafter !
But mourn,—grave, thoughtfuller souls,—till Man can view
Less Virtue marred by Vice grown overstrong,—
Less strengthless Age shorn of its reverend due,—
Or righteous Penury tasked by affluent Wrong !—
Spare mirth till, risen Christ-like, Man combines
To wrench fierce Anguish from its world-wide bed,—
To smooth the couch where sad, sick, orphanage pines,—
And feast hearts famished for life's strengthening bread !—
Refrain ! and Earth's tumultuous frets being past,
Around Heaven's Throne of Gold, wise souls, exult at last !

Two Legends of the Birth of Wine—Pro. and Con.

In the dim dead Past when the ancient Earth
Emerged from the wreck which the Deluge wrought,
(Though the sweet flowers bloomed, and the birds made mirth)
The souls of the good men saved were fraught

      With vehement trouble and thought.

For their sad hearts ached with the yearning pain
Of a passionate grief :—and their anguished groan
Beleaguered Heaven for their brethren slain :
Till the Just God,—throned on His infinite Throne—

      Arose at the multiplied moan.

And He spake :—" Let the breasts of the earth be clad
" With a gracious Gift that shall swiftly shape
" Delight from Woe !—let the world grow glad
" When the hills, and the vales, and the plains, bedrape

      " Their bountiful tracts with the grape."

At His Word sprang vines —and the mourners pressed
The plump round clusters (mellow and bright)
And quaffed, anon, with a strong, keen, zest,

And laughed with joy,—for a great delight
      Lay coiled in the red Wine's might!

Yea, the boon brought bliss to those straitened souls:—
Loud griefs grew dumb; and austere desires
Perished! And now, while the round world rolls,
Man laughs as he quaffs; and, when earth expires,
      Shall quaff and laugh mid its fires!

SECOND LEGEND.—*Con*

In the vigorous years when the Lord God's breath
Rolled pulsing life through the stagnant slime—
The moist world woke from its swoon of death
And flourished anew, as of old, ere Crime
      Had ruined its fair first prime.

But the Arch-fiend stealthily stalked from Hell
Fiercely athirst for the new World's fall,—
And vengefully sought for some fraudful spell
To craftily fashion,—and, therewithal,
      Transmute Man's honey to gall.

Then he gathered the bones of the lewd men drowned,
And sowed strange venom through and through,
And hid them, again, in the fruitful ground,
From whence, in a breath-space, upward grew
      Strong vines of a bright green hue.

Anon,—made fat with the milk o' the earth

To the prodigal plants rich fruitage clung,

And the Arch-fiend laughed with a pitiless mirth

As the ripe globes glittered :—and lo, from his tongue,

This mystical chant was sung .—

(CHANT.)

I.

" *When the Monarch, Man, by his Moulder's Hand,*

" *Was dowered with the lordship of sea and land—*

" *All gifts and growths of the herbaged soil*

" *Were his—to sustain, or spoil,—*

" *But the grape i' the Garden's midst did stand,* *

" *To Eve, and her unborn offspring, banned,—*

" *For a Menacing God, with His whirlwind-breath*

" *Had guerdoned the taste with death.*"

II.

" *But I compassed the plant with my mightiest snares*

" *And strove to entrap weak Eve unawares;*

" *Till the strength and skill of my cunning sleights*

" *Robbed Man of his pure delights.*

---

* It will be remembered that the first historic mention of Wine is in the earlier part of Genesis, and that the nature of the " forbidden fruit" of that Book is a matter of theological speculation. I have availed myself of these circumstances.

" Then vanished Peace, for the wronged God hurled

" His recreant slaves from their Eden-World —

" Where Seraph-watchers, with swords of flame—

*   " Kept guard till the Deluge came ! "*

III.

" Once again, do the Earth's lips lightly part,

" And fruitful vines through the fissures start,

" Whose red blood (shrouding unnumbered woes)

*   " Shall ruffle Man's repose.*

" Till the day of Doom let it work amain

" To bind the weak with a Despot's chain ;

" Yea,—mightily tempt till it people well

*   " The spaces of barren Hell."*

He ceased :— for the hate of his grievous ban

Was housed in the heart of the ripened vine,

To rain sharp sorrow on suffering Man,

Till the grace and love of a Power Divine

        Divorce Man's spirit from Wine.

Out of the Depths.

(TO MY WIFE.)

Ye melancholy thoughts that surge
    And breathe of days and nights engloomed—
Ye heavy hours that seem the dirge
    Of buried bliss that Time hath tombed—
Reveal—if soothing Peace is shrined
    Within the hid hereafter years,—
To murmur to my aching mind
    Delicious respite to my tears

Years twenty-nine to-night have fled
    And floated down life's Marah-stream—
But ah, their mournful months have sped
    Divested of one gladsome dream ,—
For harboured in my soul has dwelt
    A pain that poisoned all my fate—
Transmuting joys I might have felt
    To venomed pangs more fierce than hate.

To others,—Time brings pure content,
    With tender days and tranquil nights,
And joys that find an envied vent
    In visioned dreams of soft delights—

But, knowing nought of griefs that roll,
   Their solitude is not made bleak
By wintry thoughts that chill the soul,
   And clinging griefs that pale the cheek

Life teems with problems that perplex
   And plunge my soul in doubt extreme,
Existence seems ordained to vex,
   And render joy an imaged dream—
Even now, when Love—which dreamers feign
   Can lap the languid soul in bliss—
Holds masterdom within my brain—
   Its issue is a gloom like this.

Where shall I look for light? where fly
   From bitter thoughts that mar my peace?
Ah, how avoid each sombre sigh?
   How bid these restless tumults cease?
Has earth one charm? one power? one spell
   By which they may be dispossessed?
Yes—*one!* It is to dream and dwell
   Shrined on the Heaven of thy breast!

Now and Then.

(AN AUSTRALIAN SURVEY.)

I.

In dim primeval years, ere Life began,
Or fruitful earth first hailed her sovereign—Man—
Our isle lay tranced and prisoned—lapped in sleep—
Lulled by the hoarse, illimitable Deep.
Rough tempests smote her slumbers!—Seas that rolled
Stupendous waves o'erwhelmed her realms of gold!
So passed mute, mystic epochs, till she heard
Mid Ocean's psalming surge God's quickening Word.

Then, ringed with tenfold thunders, His decree
Clove the clear air, and touched the refluent sea—
Pierced through strange depths, and bade superbly rise
Earth's mightiest isle to front Heaven's balmiest skies.

Scarce pealed the mandate forth, when, straightway urged,
The broad sea shook—the quivering isle emerged—
And lo, a marvellous realm—a world new-born—
Bulked vast and void, and crowned that flood forlorn!

Awhile, great Nature drowsed.—then smiled, and graced
With myriad shapes of life that monstrous waste :—
Our skies she blessed—and bade our winds waft health—
Enriched our soil, and dowered our seas with wealth—
And placed, amid our mines, unequalled ores
And priceless gifts in pure, exhaustless, stores.

   Then, splendors sprang from earth, for giant trees
Thrust forth gaunt arms that buffeted the breeze,
And plains, that gleamed with green, showed tracts impearlèd,
To graze the future flocks of half the World !

    II

Yet, like some wizard's cave in tales of yore,—
Some wondrous haunt of necromantic lore,—
Which—barred by spells—no power could pass, until
Some stronger charm had foiled that wizard's skill—
So fared thine isle, Australia ! Wrapt in glooms,
Blind Ignorance waved here her hostile plumes—
Ruled thy fair realms, and marred them, till the day
Cook's genius tracked, and smote her where she lay

Time chronicled that deed; but Fame's full blast
Shall trump reverberate praise while Time shall last !
And ah, even now, as thus my visioned eyes
Sweep through the Past, what forms, what phantoms, rise ?

Pale Memory dreams and smiles! and soon, as years
Glide, spectral, back, he comes!—the Chief appears!
Strides his loved deck, and, with intrepid ease,
Marks, once again, strange skies and chartless seas.

And like some keen, lithe, greyhound, trained to slip
Swift from the leash, so speeds, so bounds, that ship.
Fame nerves the Chief! Strong genius fires his soul!
With Hope's prophetic gift he grasps the goal
Instinctively, and grandly scans the wave,
Calm, yet triumphant—rapturous, yet grave!

League foams past league —and still, with hopeful haste,
Yoked to that vast, yet penetrable waste,
Strains the strong ship, while, tardily, each day
Creeps like a snail-paced servitor away.

But hark! what means that shout? that beckoning hand?
Joy, joy, vibrates! for volleying cries of "land"
Pierce, with transcendent transports, through and through
That famous Chief and dauntless British crew.

On, on they speed where, past bewildering brine,
Loom gradual shores that gap the smooth sea-line;
And landward yet till, echoing on the breeze,
Yon rock-surf lifts long muffled litanies.

But who shall paint? what bard shall sing? what speech
Depict the charms which glimmer past that beach?
Behold these wave-worn wanderers! To their eyes
Earth never donned such hues, nor such the skies!
Fair flowerful nooks are there,—and groves of green,
Bright hills and hollows,—slopes and plains between;
And crowning, girdling, all—Heaven's sunbright dome
Boasts bluer gulfs than skies they loved at home.

But lo, the ship is stayed.—the longboat manned :—
Cook holds the helm, and, steering toward the strand,
Shuns yon huge cliff, whose rough colossal crest,
Massive and scarred, half-shades grey Ocean's breast,—
Grounds in yon land-locked bay, and, leaping down,
Claims there this priceless gem of Britain's crown.

III

Thus History sings!

     Since that eventful day
Ten decades, aye eleven, have passed away,
And ten, and more, since Death, close-leagued with Hate,
Adjudged heroic Cook a martyr's fate,—
While, wailing loud by Polynesia's wave,
Grief rained immortal laurels on his grave.

Aye, years have rolled between ; but ah, what pen
Shall bridge Time's broad abyss 'twixt Now and Then ?
Yea, who shall tell ? or, in exalted strains,
Chant ? how the Curse shrank backward from our plains,—
Scared by the Chief who braved the untravelled sea
And found new homes, new havens for the free ?

How swift that change !   One century back, no corn
Yellowed our unploughed plains, and fields forlorn ;
And Toil's glad voice, and sweet Devotion's psalm,
Alike unknown, had never blessed that calm ;
For Silence and Neglect had made the land
Accursed, though fair—though beautiful, yet banned.

Yes, magical that change ! Now, far and near,
Life, Culture, Commerce, Art, and Wealth appear !
Now Science, raptured, lifts her starlike eyes,
Springs from the world, and communes with the skies !
Now Commerce thrives , and now, with sunburnt brow,
Fearless and frank, Toil triumphs with his plough !
Now, with delight, see—pulsing through the land—
Vast waves of Progress day by day, expand !
Till, year by year, the bold backwoodsman's axe
Frights, with new fears, remoter hordes of blacks,
And speeds the glorious day this isle shall be
One grand Dominion—thronged from sea to sea !

Those times approach.—for lo, when British hearts
Brought Wealth and Toil that built our first fair marts,
And, rapt by these, and conquests yet to come,
Hope grew, at last, oracular, not dumb—
Swift from this coast, where Cook so well began,
Man's colonising zeal, like watchfires, ran
From point to point, till now, 'neath Heaven's sweet smile,
Seven nascent nations belt or bound this isle

IV.

Here shines our own.—young Mother of them all —
Six decades since, Tasmania, at her call,
Quick to respond, rose, vigorous at birth,
Heard the next mandate summon distant Perth;
Marked how a third, by Heaven's propitious aid,
Rolled fast and far, and quickened Adelaide,
And, how a mightier yet, past Ocean's verge,
Found brave New Zealand listening, rimmed with surge.

As giants thrive, thrived these, and, meanwhile, lo,
Victoria, Queensland, caught in turn the glow!
Till, in the north, where Day, with flaming glance,
Breeds strange rich growths in fierce luxuriance—
And, in the south, where each fan breeze that blows,
Chants dim delicious songs of distant snows,—

'Two States upsprang, and, by the names they bore,
Proved Austral hearts were British to the core.

v.

What land boasts nobler gifts?   Methinks, with hum,
That hints supreme surprise, far nations come!
With lyric lips, their glad propitious hosts
Attest what grandeur glimmers round our coasts—
Trace, in To-day's magnificent increase,
Our bloodless triumphs reaped from fields of Peace—
And, shadowed by their monarchs, marvelling stand
And hail thy gracious growth, fair Austral land!

See, high amid their throng, august, serene,—
In grace unmatched—in port, a peerless queen—
Fair England stands! and ah, our Mother's face,
With stately pride transfigured, greets the race
That faced strange skies, and combated strange foam,
To build, mid tracts remote, bold Freedom's home,—
And guard, for Austral myriads, yet to be,
The Briton's birthright,—godlike Liberty!—

Next glides a Form, colossal and apart,
Whose frank calm smile proclaims her frank calm heart:
A Power of sovereign strength, whose frame, of old,
Sprang, sinewy-limbed, from Britain's grandest mould

Scars seamed her limbs long since, when bright blood ran
And vengeful swords smote swords, and fought for Man !
But now, those feuds have perished ! Now, made free,
Priestess of Peace, and type of Unity,
She queens the Great Republic on whose sides
Two whirling Oceans plunge tumultuous tides!
Hark ! how her welcoming voice smites hill and vale
And wafts abroad the benison—" *All hail !*"

Behind this matchless vanguard, led by France,
Old Europe's kingdoms cluster, and advance.
Gaul, Austrian, Teuton,—Belgian, Swiss, and Dane,
With mingling acclamations, haste amain,
And Italy, re-risen, and throned in might,
Beholds, and comes, and kindles with delight.

Nor these alone ! The sound, the summons, hurled
By Fame's awakening trump, has pierced the world,—
And, past crowned Europe's phalanx, lo ! more swift,
More bright than noon-day clouds, that dream and drift,
I see, begemmed with spoils from mart and mine,
Thy form, Japan, and, jewelled India, thine !

VI

Nor yet, alone, throng these ! With rhythmic tread,
Lured by the chant, glide past—our hallowed dead !

Our dear illustrious dead—a kingly band—
Whose patriot-lives showered glory on the land!
And chief in fame, and foremost in the van,
Great Wentworth shines!—that lion-souled old man!—
Lordly his smile, as when—in days of old—
Thought's lightnings lit those lips, alas, now cold;
Dauntless his mien, as when—with matchless might—
He crushed the Wrong, and thundered for the Right.

O, mightiest of our dead, whose voice once awed
Corruption, and abashed both Force and Fraud—
Whose brain of splendid power, and speech of strength
Impelled our land, self-ruled,* to rise at length—
Dumb be my lips when I disown that debt!
Mute be my Muse, if, recreant, she forget!
Maimed be the song, and palsied fall the verse
That leave unpraised the name I now rehearse!

And though, my Wentworth, none as yet essays
To mould, in flawless bronze, thy faultless praise—
Sleep on! that day shall dawn! Soon, soon shall Fame
With monumental sculptures grace thy name.—
While, ranked next Cook's thy finished work shall stand!
His genius found, but thine upbuilt, our land.

---

* Note.—It will of course be remembered that Wentworth was the author of
our Constitution Act

Adieu, majestic shades, mid whose bright band
Glide Wentworth, Windeyer, Cowper, Lang, and Bland!
August your arms! exalted were the powers
That wrought brave deeds which make the Future ours!
And, as the grand grave Seer, by Heaven's command,
Surveyed, from Pisgah's crest, the Promised Land,—
Scanned that rich realm, and viewed those vales and streams,
Which oft, mid desert-griefs, had charmed his dreams,—
So, from our Pisgah-summit, round whose peak
Fame shines to-day,—what prophet-voices speak!

The Future gleams—the Present shrinks away—
And bright—past Time's dim gulf—I see that day,
When North and South—throughout this broad Isle's girth,
And East and West—from Sydney even to Perth—
Shall laugh with life's best gifts, while Wealth's increase
Crowns Virtue with Prosperity and Peace!

Australia and England.

(A Fragment for Music)

INTRODUCTION.

Lift up triumphant strains!   Let lyre and voice
Ring out rich choral anthems, and rejoice—
For lo! the dayspring spreads, till baffled night
Rolls vanquished from thy realms, O land of light!
And Fame's majestic sun climbs Heaven to shed
Divine meridian splendors on thine head!

      Chant, trumpet-tongued! and smite, from harps of gold,
Loud, sevenfold salutations! for, behold,
With hands outstretched, the world's great Nations meet
And shower imperial greetings at thy feet!

I.

In the darkness of eras unknown—
In the calm of the epochs of old—
When our fields were unploughed and unsown
And, like misers, mines hoarded their gold—
Through this realm slept a Silence, unstirred
By the music of rifle or axe,
And no song but the song of the bird
Broke the clamor of brutes and of blacks.

But those kings of the seas, and the lands—
Bold Britons—came hither to dwell—
With the strength as of gods in their hands
And the wills that command and compel—
As they come, lo, the wilderness glows!—
All our waterways whiten with ships!—
And the desert blooms out like the rose
With the Spring's soft salute on her lips!

II

Yes, when our Fathers gathered—swift as thought—
Hand leagued with hand—with craftsman craftsman wrought!
Day linked with day—and, flashing far and bright—
Toil's restless splendors beaconed busy night!
Then home upreared past home, and, crowning those,
Town grew by town, by city city rose—
Till, to the chant from Freedom's voice that rang
Titanic from its youth our Nation sprang!

III.

Yet ah, as lovers—pent in isles
Where beauty blooms mid birds and flowers—
Lament, with sighs, the scenes and smiles
That lured to bliss in happier hours—

So,—dowered with gifts—yet placed afar—
We—vassals of a Mightier Will,—
Waft tributes of our love, for ah,

    Our hearts are England's still

IV.

And, hence, as with souls leal and loyal, with hearts frank and free,
We exult, O our mother most loyal, rejoicing in thee!
Be thou queen! and let chiefs of all nations, august though they seem,
Dwindle down and descend from their stations, and waste like a
    dream!
We are fair, but thy beauty is fairer, thy love fairer still—
And our fate in thy fate shall be sharer as ages fulfil—
For thy strength like the strength of the morning shall faint not
    nor fail,
But increase as the day from the dawning!— Hail England!
    all hail!
Be thy love like a buckler before us, and none shall assail!
While thy sons chant with jubilant chorus—"Hail, England!—
    all hail"!

Song

MY QUEEN OF DREAMS

In the warm flushed heart of the rose-red West,
When the great sun quivered and died to-day,
You pulsed, O star, by yon pine-clad crest—
And throbbed till the bright eve ashened grey—

     Then I saw you swim
     By the shadowy rim
Where the grey gum dips to the western plain,
     And you rayed delight
     As you winged your flight
To the mystic spheres where your kinsmen reign!

O star, did you see her?   My queen of dreams!
Was it you that glimmered the night we strayed
A month ago by these scented streams?
Half-checked by the litter the musk-buds made?

     Did you sleep or wake?—
     Ah, for love's sweet sake,
(Though the world should fail, and the soft stars wane!)
     I shall dream delight
     Till our souls take flight
To the mystic spheres where your kinsmen reign!

Quis Separabit?

Heart clings to heart! Let the strange years sever
The fates of two who have met to part—
Love's strength survives, and the harsh world never
Shall crush the passion of heart for heart!
For I know my life, though it droop and dwindle,
Shall leave me love, till I fade and die;
And when hereafter, our souls rekindle,
Who shall be fonder, you or I?

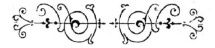

F W WHITE,
MARKET STREET WEST,
SYDNEY

CPSIA information can be obtained
at www.ICGtesting.com
Printed in the USA
BVHW010303070622
638998BV00023B/43